# EX CATHEDRA

## XXVI

PETER JOANNIDES

Printed in the United States of America

Corrected second printing, 2019

ISBN 978-0-9892536-9-7

www.PetroulisI@gmail.com

# AUTHOR'S NOTE

This is the latest in the series of **Ex Cathedras** begun in 1972.

## A Long-due Acknowledgement

I wish to express here my gratitude and appreciation to George Hiscock for his counsel, assistance, support, and innumerable editorial labors he has bequeathed me, not only for this volume of **Ex Cathedras**, but also for **all** of my previous work, which includes my Magnum Opus **Amán Amán!** as well as all subsequent **Ex Cathedras** from **Ex Cathedra IX** to **Ex Cathedra XXV**.

Without his help, I doubt if any of my work would have come to fruition.


I would also like to take this occasion to thank Herb Sussman for all his efforts on my behalf in terms of advice, editing, and proofreading throughout **all** my writing history. Also to Maya Joannides for her suggestions and careful reviewing of many of my later **Ex Cathedras**.

Certain acknowledgements should have been made at the time of the publication of **Amán Amán!** as well. I would like to rectify this omission. The following individuals were significantly instrumental in making **Amán Amán!** a better and more error-free book: Michele Johnson, Charles Moore, Robert Bryan, Matthew Schultz, David Smith;
and Andy Dellis and John Georgiou for helping me navigate through the transliterating quandary of Modern Greek.

Peter Joannides

ALSO BY PETER JOANNIDES

*Amán Amán!*
*Ex Cathedras (IX-XV)*
*More Ex Cathedras (XVI-XXII)*
*Ex Cathedra XXIII*
*Ex Cathedra XXIV*
*Ex Cathedra XXV*

*March 15, 2017*

# *Ex*
# *Cathedra*

## 26th
## Encyclical

**von Herrn Doktor Professor Peter Joannides**

1

My mind can't take anymore in; it's starting to leak things out.

Being an old geographical hand, dams (and their ensuing jumbo lakes), as well as artificial islands, make me feel a bit uncomfortable.

Every book that's ever been published has been aspectual.

Except mine.

4

There is an underlying wisdom and common humanity harbored in the political cartoon.

I have this stupid daydream:

An experimenter gathers a random number of pedestrians wearing wrist watches, including me, and then instructs each one to signal when a certain exact time occurs to see who will come closest to the actual, schizotrichiatric, Observatory-measured time.

And, of course, I win hands down.

6

When something is good, I don't mind eating it twice in a row.

I don't know about thrice.

There is such a thing as terribly private jokes that can only be understood by oneself.

8

So many things I didn't do that I thought I would do.

A hallowed memory: On the way to Staten Island and The Farm, the squeal of the South Ferry local after we changed trains at Chambers Street.

Aging is so inexorable and **gradual**, and is only fully realized at the tail end.

The homogenization of peoples, cultures, races means the mishmash of language.

And yet…

12

Prague, Bratislava, Budapest:  the sea nowhere in sight, the somewhat insipid customs, the stultifying furnitures, the gothic and baroque disfigurements and architectural curlicues…

Not my sort of places.

13

I've read or heard somewhere that the Indians called it firewater.

What an apt name!

I now see so many of my experiences as eternal tableaus of space-time.

Why couldn't I have seen them that way **then**?

"Do some of the higher animals know they're going to die?"

No doubt this would be fodder for the analytic philosophers with their definitions, subtle distinctions, and pedantries.

But it's still an interesting question.

16

If I become the Planetary Dictator, I think I will probably make Obama President-for-Life.

Côte d'Azur

Weary, Weary, Weary.

18

Miami Beach, Virginia Beach, Rimini, Brighton…

Just as weary.

19

Can you imagine what Oman was like in 1910?

Whenever I see pictures, documentaries, travelogues, tourist itineraries… of Scandinavia, it always seems to be summertime.

21

Cars of the 50's with enormous wide bodies, gigantic fins, garish ornaments, and sleeky stripes... now look ridiculous and absurd.

Perhaps even grotesque.

What is the difference between an **Americanítha** and an **Americána**?

Between an **Americanós** and an **Americános**?

Those in-the-know know.

I wonder what the Caribbean Arawaks were really like.

Was there ever a gentle people on this planet?

24

Headscarves are nothing less than a goddam **uniform**.

I don't know why, but they irritate me no end.

"To **distill**" is now paramount and of the essence.

Hari Sreenivasan

Every long once in a while somebody appears on TV that you just **know** is a good and decent person.

27

## The Incredible Shrinking Man

The wondrous and mystic ending.  It's happening.

Analogously perhaps, but it's happening.

## The Internet

I never dreamed that one day I would have the World at my fingertips.

I know of no country in the world other than the United States where, while driving, one has to hide a flask of spirits in the trunk of his car like a goddam sneak thief.

A repeat.

I don't mind driving a car with here and there a few scratches, but absolutely **no dents**.

How can there be a **then** and how can there be a **now**?  Then and now.  A strange connection and unfathomable mystery.

I often think of those halcyon days in Rhodos when every day at lunch I would have my little half-litre bottle of CAIR retsina.

Looking through an old address book: what stings and dead-end culverts of time.

34

It's a good thing that the irreversible and lethal pill is not readily available, because if it were, there were innumerable times when I would have used it.

I wonder if there is anyone in the world who has a lower threshold of pain than I.

It is a lot easier and less troublesome to just follow the rules.

37

A droll and unforgettable line from **The African Queen**: "By the authority vested in me by Kaiser Wilhelm II I pronounce you man and wife proceed with the execution."

38

When I was young, all the things that were going on that I hadn't the foggiest inkling of.

Ethiopians are a handsome people.

It would be wonderful to be able to speak French, but I'd rather be able to speak Italian, Spanish, German, Arabic, Turkish, Portuguese, Swahili, Russian, Hindi… beforehand.

41

To desert from an army run by mindless officers answerable to mindless politicians answerable to mindless autocrats is in fact a virtue.

One of the wittiest names for a Dick Tracy villain:

B.O. Plenty

## 43

Structures, Structures! I can't tell you how blissful it is to contemplate Structures.

I've given up trying to be consistent.

I wish **I** could have come up with a line like this:

"Candy is dandy but liquor is quicker."

Ocean liners, aircraft carriers, nuclear submarines, oil rigs:  universes in miniature.

## # 42

A close second:  Pruneface.

48

## Charles de Gaulle

Can you imagine the gall of de Gaulle, an invited guest of a sovereign nation, publicly encouraging one of its provinces to secede.

49

One of the terrible things about writing is that you can't undo what you've written.

## Beauty

A little flick of fuchsia-red in a sea of green.

Eulogies are off-putting; they invariably distort.

## Actors

Just knowing that someone is **acting** is deflating enough.

53

If there's anything that disgusts me and makes me want to puke, it's when wild animals are made to dance, pirouette, and burlesque in fairs and circuses.

I remember once passing a building (a YMCA, Health Club, Recreation Center...) where a handball tournament was going on.

A quiet building that no one would particularly take notice of.

And thinking if only a passer-by could know what struggles, exhaustions, willpowers, calculations, sweats, wrenchings, and nerves were unfolding inside.

55

What sometimes outlandish shapes and sizes human beings come in.

# # 54

And other quiet buildings, where unspeakable things were going on.

No more 7th Game of the World Series, Super Bowls, Academy Awards, Greek Festivals, Presidential Elections, Olympic Golds, Easter Midnights, New Year's Eve Celebrations…

What's become of me?

58

Somehow, our fondest memories seem to have to do with some form of goodness.

I love eccentric old English Ladies.

60

I know so little about so many things.

And yet about so many things, I know a little.

61

When I hit a pothole, it hurts me more than it hurts my car.

Just as I relish **tempura** cooked in front of you, one morsel at a time,

So I would relish **haloúmi** fried, piece by piece.

(Fried **haloúmi** can cool off in a hurry.)

What sort of moron can sit and listen to a barking dog all day long?

64

If only the frisking young could know how lucky they are to be able to walk, to see, to hear, to smell, to taste.

65

All those people that I wanted to honor and commemorate (and to impress) with my work…

Are now mostly dead.

How delightful it is to listen to David Attenborough describe the abundance and intricacy of nature.

"Life is a sort of excrescent and filmy scum found, for brief periods, on the surface of certain minor planets."

Why is this thought so exhilarating?

## Idle Musing

How come I was born into just this particular stage of evolution, civilization, technology?

And not into some other, before or after?

It's the fifth-year anniversary of the nuclear disaster at the Fukushima Daiichi Plant in Japan.

Fifth year!

Why it was only just yesterday in the News, couldn't have been more than a few months ago!

## # 65

As well, I'm afraid, as all those paybacks.

For years I drove my car, smug and self-satisfied, without any seatbelts on.

I wonder if this sort of painful vacillation occurs to many other writers:

For example, you sometimes put in take out, put in take out, put in take out… more than several times a certain preposition, say, until you finally just have to make a decision.

The greatest line of all literature, bar none:

"There are more things in heaven and earth, Horatio, Than are dreamt of in your philosophy."

Michael Bloomberg would probably make a good President.

Some of the TV offerings—quiz shows, situation comedies, prize competitions, family entertainments—are nothing less than **INANE**.

At times I take a dislike to someone, for hardly any reasons.

I could give examples.

I have very little interest in the life of Napoleon Bonaparte.

I'm beginning to identify with all who are in pain, of whatever variety.

## Crane Flies

Delicate and gossamer, with translucent wings, soft and slow-moving, uninimical, in a word beautiful...

Believe it or not, I could even have one for a roommate. (Indoors!)

And coming from me, that's saying a lot.

I am always amazed at the endless varieties of songs and melodies that are based on a relatively limited number of tones.

(I keep asking myself why someone hadn't come up with that tune before?)

Are tones and melodies like an alphabet and words?  Or like words and literatures?

It's hard for me to believe that the analogy holds.  There doesn't seem to be that many tones and that many ways of putting them together.

But I may just be out of my element here.

My contempt and disrespect and distaste for some doctors have now come back, full force.

If the aesthetic dimension were to be found in just the colors and their juxtapositions, then I might have liked fireworks.

But I don't like fireworks.

And yet there is the Aurora Borealis.
(And snake skins and raccoon whiskers.)

Is it that I just don't like human intervention?

Rehashing old ground.

I wonder if there could be a planet peopled by creatures or intelligent inhabitants who felt pleasures of astounding variety but never any pain—in fact, would be nonplussed by the whole notion of pain?

## The World of Art

More often than not: what fraudulence, chicanery, hubris, and cant.

I find it appalling, tragic, and remarkable that so many of my cherished writers died at such an early age.

I can't get over George Orwell dying at 46.

All these female political commentators: like frantic chattering chirping birds.

Russell, always looking for absolute certainty, would explore the world of mathematics and logic.

I don't know why one has to go so far afield.

It seems to me that painfully obvious statements like "There are three pairs of socks in the second drawer" and "I have $34 in my wallet," given the ordinary meanings involved, without any sophisticated physics or epistemology, are about as certain as you can get.

(Shades of G. E. Moore.)

When reading **The New York Times,** I really don't have much use for "The Arts." Most of the time it seems like a lot of adolescent nonsense.

I can't seem to avoid repetitions. I keep forgetting that I've already said the same things before, sometimes identically so, and sometimes only in a little different way.

I apologize to the Reader.

Mankind's lowest common denominator—atrocities, tortures, severe illnesses, starvation, chronic agonies, excruciating pain—must become mankind's preeminent concern.

Given the times and my age at the time, I think perhaps the most **gripping** film I've ever seen:

**Lost Horizon**

Why isn't Lynn Bari included in the **World Almanac's** "Entertainers of the Past"?

People when televised are quite different people when not being televised.

I worry, given my sometime vulgarisms and profane and scurrilous language, that I may not be worthy of comparison to Logan Pearsall Smith.

If I had a penny from every American (and I suspect that hardly anyone would begrudge the loss of a penny), I would have $3,500,000 in my bank account.

Despite what I said about disavowing and letting go, I seem to carry my burdensome and long-lasting work with me like a carapace.

It has slowly dawned on me that a goodly portion of my writing has essentially and all along been for my dwindling generation.

And that most of its successors will probably not have the foggiest notion of much of what I have been so wrought up, absorbed, and enthusiastic about.

I don't see why a newspaper or magazine article can't continue and end more or less near where it begins, and not be referred to a way-back page, most irritating to have to shuffle, search, and get to.

There must have been something about Hilaire Belloc that I really didn't like.

But, for the life of me, I just can't remember what it is.

I have actually forgotten who some of the real-life characters in my book were.

Neil deGrasse Tyson is highly intelligent and is mostly right about what he says.

(For Kimon Friar.)

The blue of the oceans on my Atlas—so still and crystalline and pure—knows not of violent storms and giant waves, upheavals and tsunamis.

Shall we then enshrine this line from T.S. Eliot:

"And every moment is a new and shocking Valuation of all we have been."

Only God, in all of his unlimited tenure and omniscience, can truly understand and evaluate my work.

Not to take away from its obvious merit and worthiness, it's still a little bit disturbing that one can recognize a Ken Burns film within a minute or so.

## Lilac Vegetal

I remember the first barbershop with Mama, somewhere in Washington Heights.

Pre-school days.

## Lilac Vegetal

Throughout the years, years upon the years, and after-shave.

Unto this very day.

Only babies on film can't fake it.

Is it this that will be achingly remembered: the night we all drove together around the neighborhood to see the Christmas lights?

It sometimes comes as a shock when a young good-looking girl, reaching a certain middle age, suddenly becomes matronly.

Wetlands, river deltas, mangrove swamps, tropical forests, semi-deserts, Arctic and Antarctic whites, snow-topped mountain ranges, pullulating mega-cities, lucent Swiss hillsides, innumerable customs and languages, structures and networks...

What treasures on this varied planet!

So many seem to have come to some minimal understanding and accommodation with things.

I seem to keep confusedly putting two and two together right until this very day.

The thought has crossed my mind: how insensitive, self-oriented, unempathetic I sometimes was in my younger years.

(I wish I had spent more time then with my father and my Uncle John.)

.

How **narrow** our awareness was when we were younger.

Pain does not enhance one's disposition.

## 115

It's a wonder I've escaped being dispatched by some irate husband or boyfriend.

All the hygienic advice we've been handed down over the years that's turned out to be balderdash and flummery.

Opening Ceremony of the Olympics (and not just this last one).

Other than the Parade of Athletes, the rest is a self-conscious and stylized inflated embarrassing bore.

I'm beginning to have contempt for anyone who would vote for Donald Trump, including my friends.

Since everything short of tiddlywinks is represented in the Olympics, why not American (Irish) handball?

I'm all for the Olympics.

It's a remarkable tradition.

Literature, being in its original form, is the one thing that educators can't fuck up.

Every so often I come upon an obituary—that of a Dr. Donald A. Henderson who was instrumental in fully eliminating smallpox for the rest of us—and thinking that, surely, his was a life well-spent.

I sometimes wonder whether I had sense enough to bring a bottle of wine or spirits to Tasso Zafiriou for all those magnificent meals at Benguerir.

It haunts me that I would have been so insensitive not to.

It was so long ago and maybe I was so unthinking that I didn't.

But then again maybe I did.

I'd like to think that I did.

I expect my Reader to be thoroughly familiar with my work.

Doesn't it seem odd and quizzical that all the "sound and fury" of present-day elections, debates, military incursions, earthquakes, revolutions, migrations… will one day be long-ago selected photographs and summarized commentary in some future historical anthology?

Even if I say so myself, I am an expert, by feel and touch alone, on pouring just the exactly right amount of olive oil and vinegar on a green salad.

I don't like my wine **with** my food.

Not only does it interrupt, but it also sort of bites and nags at the rhythm and pleasure of my dining.

I like my wine **before** my food.

If you really want the true lowdown of a language, you have to deal with a native speaker.

I once came face-to-face with a barracuda. I don't know how much danger I was really in, but it scared the hell out of me.

I like a shower that's like a waterfall.

My friends are becoming fewer and fewer, owing to death, disappearance, distance, divergence.

People who kill elephants for sport or profit are particularly noxious.

## Archbishop Makarios

I've never before heard Greek so softly and flawlessly and elegantly pronounced.

134

It surprised me and pleased me to learn that Michael Cacoyannis was a Cypriot.

I may not have done it all, but in a way I have done it all.

Greek-Americana is neither Greek nor Americana.

137

In the end, movies, even the best of them, have in fact corrupted us.

138

"Dogs are a man's best friend."

I don't know when all this got started, but it has nothing to do with me.

I've lost interest in so many things.

I don't see why the production and dissemination of medicines shouldn't be under government mandate—without a profit motive. With researchers to be duly and well-rewarded. As well as competent doctors (within a reasonable limit).

So much for Big Pharma.

141

"A ravaging raging storm outside,

We safe and snug inside."

One of the great boons of civilization.

I am full of personal things that are too personal to be written about.

One by one, my f-a-c-u-l-t-i-e-s are deserting me.

144

I hate to say this because I was a part of it:

There is no question that Wittgenstein was a
genius, but I think perhaps the whole hullabaloo was a
bit overblown.

Someone might surmise from my writings that I am anti-French. Which isn't really true.

It's just that when all the jealousy, regret, and inability are accounted for—a big percentage—there is still some small residue left of something that is truly uncomfortable and alien.

Speaking of movies, have you ever noticed that the big super spectaculars with a cast and array of numerous superstars never seem to work out?

I wish I had done all the sexual things that I imagined.

148

I've been having strange dreams lately, of characters, events, places, habits long-forgotten.

It seems to me that CNN is probably the fairest News Service.

I've never read Tolstoy's Masterpiece, and I don't think I ever will.

Ordinal Numbers: How easy in English; how convoluted in Greek.

Sometimes I think to be a gourmet is the highest calling.

I can't think of an occupation I am less suited to than that of a dog-groomer.

When you get to my age, you no longer hold grudges.

(But I have to admit, it's a little bit hard to forget Dr. James M. Gregg of the Mayo Clinic.)

155

I'm not sure I could, or even want to, handle a smartphone.

I can't stand crowds, of **ANY** persuasion.

157

Young people have no idea of the pleasures and rewards of being a curmudgeon.

Of all the sneeze rejoinders in all this big international world, surely the most insipid must be "Bless You!"

159

Virginia Mayo in **The Best Years of Our Lives**.

Virginia Mayo recently interviewed about **The Best Years of Our Lives**.

Oh the ravages of time!

160

President Donald J. Trump:  Redneck Heaven

I love colors; I always have.

162

Even though I am a fascist, I still passionately like to see the right people elected in democracies.

I used to think Bush was bad; now I think him to have been a comparative Angel.

Yesterday, I was rummaging around an old bookstore and asked the owner if he had any old minor and out-of-the-ordinary Jules Verne books. Somehow, he unearthed for me **Master of the World** which was the sequel to **Robur the Conqueror** and which I hadn't read and was probably the last book the author ever wrote.

It was an electrifying moment for me.

I often think of some of the excellent handball players who died young (Freddie Munsch, Merc Morris, Ken Ginty…).

Writers' conferences, retreats, workshops… might **seem** to be akin to Logan Pearsall Smith's "Fine writers should split hairs together, and sit by side, like friendly apes, to pick the fleas from each other's prose," but in truth they are worlds apart.

I've never been interested in having or running a business. With this exception: A tour company that shall be called "Ultimate Tours." A **small** contingent of clients would be taken by helicopter to the most remote of remotest places, and there left with all imaginable amenities, to be picked up again after a specified time. With an attendant scientific expert (or experts) to guide and explain.

Needless to say, the fee for such an adventure would be considerably substantial. However, there would be a sliding scale of fees for those clients not so economically endowed but who would still merit such a trip on the strength of their application, and thus the very rich would offset and balance the expense. (It would be conceivable for a client to have a $0 fee.)

(The same could be done by ship, with its obvious advantages, depending, however, upon the location of the "most remote of remotest.")

Once in a while, I have used a word that I didn't really know the meaning of.

(Yet, somehow, everything turned out all right.)

(Example: "bimbo.")

No man should permit himself the indignity of watching a movie with periodic interruptions of advertisements.

Frank Sinatra wasn't a bad actor.

It would be no less than fitting for Donald J. Trump to experience waterboarding.

Whatever and whomever Donald Trump likes or admires—I do not like, and do not admire.

173

Now that Obama is fit and experienced and honed to have a few more years as President, it's a shame he no longer can be.

I'd love to visit islands like Mayotte.

(It's too bad that so many are under the French mantle.)

Now that it's come to my attention and I have finally figured things out, I'll be damned if I will give the Turks the satisfaction of naming my old and dear friend Costa's hometown (of Asia Minor and pre-Kemal days) "**Kirmasti**" instead of its proper Greek name of "**Kremasti**."

(Note the changes that need to be made in **Ex Cathedra XXI # 166**, and in **Aman Aman!** pp. 292, 960, and 1170, Amazon Editions.)

## A Scenario


Vastly superior Aliens visit our planet and decide to invest power in one benevolent individual, and then no longer interfere.

The one individual would be given the power of being invincible to death or disease (assassination, accident, sickness, etc.) for a specified time, and also the power of being able to inflict headache/nausea (from relatively mild to very **very** intense) on any individual, group, or whole population, with the ability to inflict and rescind at will. After a sufficiently long tenure, he would be able to transfer this power to a successor.

Given the right individual, the Planet would soon be set straight.

Most people don't deserve the technology at their beck and call.

Why, during so many years, year after year after year, why oh why did I not use an electric shaver?

I love people who go out of their way to be correct and exact.

Israel, right or wrong!

Isn't it so, Jewish (**Democratic**) Senators Schumer, Blumenthal, Wyden.

It's a good thing there are principled individuals in government like Senator Dianne Feinstein.

Donald Trump

Vulgarity oozes out from his every pore.

Checks, credit cards, debit cards, money orders notwithstanding, I love **cash**, and I hope it is never eliminated.

Sex is so imperious, that it blots out everything else.

But once it is consummated, everything else blots it out.

In the end, everything that has been said has become a cliché, including this very remark itself.

I'm terrified of chronic physical pain.

If I **had** to put a label on myself, I guess "scientific humanist" wouldn't be too far off the mark.

Donald Trump

Don't ever expect a "Mr. President" from me, wise-ass.

No more lectures; there has to be pictures.

Mencken was right about the booboisee; just witness the last election.

I'd like to, in the middle of the Amazon rain forest, get into some extraordinary but comfortable suit that would be impervious to attack by any animal or plant, however large or however small, and still be able to amble about and see, hear, and smell.

I can handle a little bit of pain, but not a whole lot.

A few years back, I went to see an old friend in Kifisia. She didn't want to spend the little time we had cooking, and so she told me that she was taking me out to a restaurant for lunch.

We had a pleasant time, and as I was about to board the train for central Athens, I had the distinct and foreboding feeling that I was never to see her again.

And so it has been. I never again saw her, or even talked to her one last time on the telephone.

193

A true dilemma:  I don't know which I relish more—oysters or scallops.

Three of the most astounding experiences of my life:

When I first came upon the 1920 edition of Bartholomew's **The Times Atlas of the World** at the Library of Congress.

When I first saw the 32" illuminated Replogle Globe.

When I received the Fifth and final Volume of the Mid-Century edition of Bartholomew's **The Times Atlas of the World**, mailed to me in Jacksonville and picked up at a building, I don't remember exactly where, but I think somewhere on Hendricks Avenue near the railroad tracks, not far from San Marco.

The last beggars description—it cannot be compared to anything else, before or after. I felt utterly purified, transfigured, and remade—perhaps comparable to what Larry experienced on top of the Tibetan mountain in **The Razor's Edge**.

## Donald Trump

Civilization suddenly took a wrong turn.

Memory does play tricks, and sometimes can be awfully mistaken.

There must be devised a method of killing the animals that we consume with the least possible instance of pain.

(As much as it would dearly cost me, I am willing to forego foie gras.)

I'm waiting for The Aliens to have me take over.

Only self-propelled artists don't have bosses.

In the end I forgive everyone, for, as Maigret undoubtedly mused, no one really had any choice in the matter.

www.ingramcontent.com/pod-product-compliance
Lightning Source LLC
Chambersburg PA
CBHW071959040426
42447CB00009B/1407